CHRISTINA APPLEGATE

The Unscripted Journey of a Comedy Legend

SCOTT RODMAN

Copyright @ 2024 By Mattie Snow

All rights reserved. No part of this book may be reproduced, distributed, or transmitted in any form or by any means, including photocopying, recording, or other electronic or mechanical methods, without the prior written permission of the publisher, except in the case of brief quotations embodied in critical reviews and specific other noncommercial uses permitted by copyright law.

Contents

INTRODUCTION

CHAPTER 1: EARLY DAYS

   Family Background and Early Influences

   The Spark of Performance: First Steps into Acting

CHAPTER 2: BREAKTHROUGH ROLE

   The Role of Kelly Bundy: "Married with Children"

   Navigating Fame and Its Challenges

CHAPTER 3: THE TRANSITION TO FILM

   From Television to the Big Screen

   Key Roles and Career Highlights

CHAPTER 4: EMBRACING CHANGE

   Exploring New Genres: Drama and Adventure

   Collaborations with Renowned Directors

CHAPTER 5: PERSONAL STRUGGLES

   Battling Personal Challenges and Health Issues

   The Importance of Support Systems

CHAPTER 6: A NEW CHAPTER

   Becoming a Mother: Balancing Career and Family

   Finding Strength in Vulnerability

CHAPTER 7: ADVOCACY AND AWARENESS
- Raising Awareness for Breast Cancer
- Empowering Others Through Personal Experience

CHAPTER 8: RETURNING TO COMEDY
- The Success of "Dead to Me"
- Reinventing Comedy in a New Era

CHAPTER 9: LIFE BEYOND ACTING
- Business Ventures and Production Work
- Philanthropy and Giving Back

CHAPTER 10: LEGACY AND INFLUENCE
- Christina's Impact on Comedy and Culture
- Inspiration for Future Generations

CONCLUSION

INTRODUCTION

Christina Applegate's career path in entertainment is proof of her talent, tenacity, and the healing power of humor. Christina was born in Hollywood, California, on November 25, 1971. Her parents are record producer Robert Applegate and actress and singer Nancy Priddy. She was raised surrounded by the vibrant culture of Hollywood and her mother's career, and she was steeped in the arts from a young age. Her love of performing was sparked by her unusual upbringing, which inspired her to pursue acting wholeheartedly.

Christina first gained notoriety as a young performer, appearing in several TV series and advertisements. When she was chosen to play Kelly Bundy in the popular comedy "Married with Children" in 1987, it became her breakthrough role. After airing for over ten years, the program became a cultural phenomenon and cemented Christina's place in the public eye. As the cheerful yet relatively innocent Bundy, she demonstrated her comic skill and built a rapport with the viewers. The character's outlandish actions and catchy one-liners became classic moments, and Christina's portrayal won her praise from critics and opened doors for her subsequent pursuits.

Following the success of "Married with Children," Christina made a seamless move into the film and television industries. Her versatility as an actress proved in films such as "Don't Tell Mom the Babysitter's Dead" (1991) and "The Sweetest Thing" (2002), where she showcased her comic acting versatility. She immediately became a highly sought-after star in Hollywood thanks to her captivating appearance and sharp wit. She accepted jobs that required greater complexity and demonstrated her dramatic abilities while still receiving praise for them.

Christina's voyage was not without difficulties, though. She received a breast cancer diagnosis in 2008, which marked a sea change in her life that affected both her personal and professional life. Christina took on the challenge head-on and used her experience to advocate for breast cancer support and awareness rather than letting this disease define her. After undergoing therapy and a double mastectomy, she not only survived the disease but also became a strong advocate for others impacted by it. Her honesty in her battles with health and body image struck a chord with many people, inspiring her.

Christina has been defying expectations in recent years. She returned to the small screen in the critically praised Netflix series "Dead to Me." She co-stars with Linda Cardellini in this dark comedy, which uses humor and compassion to explore themes of friendship, loss, and life's intricacies. Christina has received additional critical acclaim and demonstrated her growth as an actress with her depiction of Jen Harding, a woman coping with betrayal and sorrow. She can explore more intense emotional tales and showcase her humorous skills on the show, further solidifying her reputation as a versatile actor.

Beyond her career successes, Christina has shared her experiences with anxiety and sadness to advocate for mental health awareness. Her frank talks about these problems have aided in dispelling the stigma associated with mental health, inspiring others to get treatment and be open about their difficulties. Christina exemplifies resilience through her advocacy activities, showing that vulnerability can be an asset.

As we delve into Christina Applegate's life and career, we will examine the critical junctures that molded her, from her early days in Hollywood to her on-screen successes and her support of significant causes. This book will emphasize her steadfast resolve, capacity for growth and adaptation, and the humor that has characterized her career. This is the tale of a lady who has not only become a comedy star but also an iconic figure in the entertainment industry, navigating life's obstacles with humor and elegance.

Examining Christina Applegate's life allows one to see the person behind the jokes and celebrate her successes while recognizing her challenges. Readers will discover the true meaning of a comic legend via this voyage, which is full of humor, resiliency, and the steadfast power of optimism.

CHAPTER 1: EARLY DAYS

Family Background and Early Influences

Long before Christina Applegate came into the spotlight, her path into the entertainment industry started. Her early life was filled with creativity and inspiration because she was born into a family with strong ties to the performing arts. The gifted actress and singer Nancy Priddy was well-known for her roles in TV shows like "Days of Our Lives" and "The Twilight Zone." Throughout her career, Priddy showed her talent and greatly impacted Christina. Christina's interest in acting was sparked by the energy and excitement of the entertainment industry, which she was exposed to growing up. She frequently went to film sets and rehearsals with her mother.

Even though Christina grew up in Hollywood, she faced difficulties as a child. When she was very young, her mother became a single parent after her parents divorced. This shift impacted Christina's perspective on adult relationships and family dynamics. Nancy put in a lot of effort to provide for Christina and her brother, frequently balancing the duties of parenthood with her acting career. Christina learned perseverance and tenacity from watching her mother overcome the challenges of being a single mother while following her vocation. Christina's professional path would be built upon her strong work ethic and dedication to her trade.

Christina started to develop a natural talent for performing in her early years. She launched her career at age five when she landed a commercial job, her first acting venture. This early achievement gave her a taste of the acting business and bolstered her self-assurance. At six years old, Christina had landed a part in "Days of Our Lives," playing Billie Reed. She gained priceless knowledge about the business via her work on the soap opera, including the value of timing, discipline, and the nuances of performing in front of the camera. Her participation in the show sharpened her acting abilities and expanded her comprehension of the subtle emotional aspects needed for different parts.

Her love of acting grew as she grew older, spurred on by her involvement in school plays and community theater. These early performances enhanced her versatility as an actress and allowed her to experiment with various personalities and genres. She thrived in the nurturing environment of Hollywood High School, where she engaged in theater activities that further honed her craft. She started embracing her distinct voice and artistic personality during this time in her life, characterized by her growing confidence.

Her family influenced Christina, but she also idolized several celebrities who served as role models. She looked up to Meryl Streep's dramatic depth and Goldie Hawn's comedic timing, hoping to infuse her own performances with a similar mix of humor and pathos. This inspired Christina to approach her work honestly and create characters who connected with viewers on a personal level.

Christina also had to deal with the difficulties of growing up in the spotlight, even at a young age. As she became more well-known for her parts, celebrity demands affected her life. She had to learn to blend the demands of acting with the normal experiences of puberty to navigate these hurdles, which required maturity beyond her years. Christina has the skills necessary to manage the challenges of her chosen vocation because of her early exposure to celebrity and her mother's mentoring.

The Spark of Performance: First Steps into Acting

Christina Applegate's career began with a spark that kindled her early interest in acting, leading to a bright and diversified career. Surrounded by the energy and excitement of the entertainment business, she grew up in

Los Angeles, a city entirely of artistic options. Christina's fascination with acting was sparked by her mother, Nancy Priddy's career as an actress and singer.

She received her first commercial appearance at the age of five. With this chance, she made her first steps into the performing industry and experienced the thrill of being in front of the camera. Despite its small size, the job ignited her acting interest and gave her insight into the entertainment industry. She cherished the creative expression and rush of performance, and this experience prepared her for her future pursuits.

Christina was encouraged to pursue possibilities in school performances and local theater while she pursued her passion for performing. She landed a role on the venerable daytime serial opera "Days of Our Lives," where she played Billie Reed by the time she was six years old. This was a crucial event for her early career because it allowed her to collaborate with seasoned pros and learn so much about the nuances of acting. She knew the value of quick memory, emotional honesty, and the capacity to express complex emotions in a condensed amount of time from the fast-paced nature of soap operas.

While filming for "Days of Our Lives," Christina rapidly learned the industry's necessity for discipline and professionalism. Her career would benefit significantly from her ability to retain focus and give consistent performances, which the demanding shooting schedules required. In addition to honing her acting skills, her time in the soap opera expanded her knowledge of the behind-the-scenes workings of television production, providing her with a holistic perspective of crafting gripping stories.

Christina's early participation in community theater allowed her to explore various genres outside of her television work. She participated in regional plays, which boosted her self-assurance and increased her acting range. These encounters allowed her to try various parts and performing philosophies, which helped her define her artistic approach and reaffirm her love of acting.

She was motivated by her involvement in community theater and the portrayals of other actors she found admirable. Observing their efforts stoked her desire and inspired her to go beyond what she thought was possible. The likes of Goldie Hawn and Meryl Streep inspired her to combine humor with profundity in her performances, which eventually resulted in the development of her own performing style.

Christina's commitment to acting became increasingly evident as she entered her teenage years. She committed herself to honing her trade, embracing its pleasures and obstacles. Her dedication paid off when she was cast as a lead in the popular sitcom Married with Children, which debuted in 1987 at the age of sixteen. Her portrayal of Kelly Bundy was a major turning point in her career, propelling her into a celebrity.

CHAPTER 2: BREAKTHROUGH ROLE

The Role of Kelly Bundy: "Married with Children"

When Christina Applegate was cast as Kelly Bundy in the ground-breaking sitcom "Married with Children," her career dramatically shifted in 1987. Michael G. Moye and Ron Leavitt created the sitcom, which followed the dysfunctional Bundy family's misadventures, including Ed O'Neill's character Al, Katey Sagal's character Peggy, and their two kids, Kelly and Bud. At sixteen, Christina took on the position of the adolescent daughter, which turned out to be one of her most memorable roles.

Kelly Bundy was described as the classic "dumb blonde," possessing a combination of audacity and innocence that both delighted and irritated her family.

The character was well-known for her extravagant wardrobe choices, flirty demeanor, and glaring lack of common sense, frequently resulting in humorous situations. Despite these shortcomings, Kelly's charisma and self-assurance won over viewers, solidifying her status as a revered figure in television history. Christina's portrayal of Kelly was crucial in making her a cultural figure in the late 1980s and early 1990s.

Christina Applegate embraced the humorous aspects of the part right away, demonstrating her superb timing and punchline delivery skills. In several instances, she skilfully blended moments of unexpected depth with Kelly's ditzy character, showcasing her comedic abilities. Christina's innate sense of humor was frequently capitalized on by the show's writers, who allowed her to excel in numerous memorable plots. Kelly stood out as a character in the series because of her unique combination of personality and humor.

Christina was also able to play a variety of comic situations. Whether it was Kelly's ridiculous dating endeavors, her ignorance of family issues, or her never-ending plans to avoid accountability, Christina's performances were distinguished by a distinct charm that won over viewers. Her portrayal and the show's irreverent humor stretched boundaries and offered a novel perspective on family interactions, upending the conventions of the era's sitcoms.

"Married with Children" attracted a devoted following and received critical praise during its run, turning it into a cultural phenomenon. Throughout the show's 11 seasons, Christina cemented her reputation as a gifted actor in Hollywood. In addition to helping her start her career, Kelly Bundy's role gave her invaluable experience in front of the camera because comedy production is a fast-paced setting that calls for flexibility and rapid thinking.

Christina received numerous nominations and honors for her work as Kelly Bundy, including a Young Artist Award and multiple nominations for Emmy Awards. She soon established herself as one of the show's most notable stars when her performance struck a chord with viewers. Christina's portrayal of Kelly Bundy demonstrated her capacity to combine sensitivity and humor, which helped her establish a personal connection with the audience.

Even though the part was humorous, Christina had difficulties as she grew from adolescence to maturity in the character of Kelly. Christina's ambition to play more serious roles occasionally conflicted with the character's image as a carefree teenager. However, she made the most of her time on the show to hone her skills and get recognition from a large audience, which opened doors for her future professional endeavors.

Christina Applegate became well-known as "Married with Children" ended in 1997, largely because of her portrayal of Kelly Bundy. The character significantly impacted how comparable archetypes were portrayed on television in the future. Because of her work on the show, Christina could explore various roles in television and movies that demonstrated her range as an actor, which paved the way for her future success in Hollywood.

Navigating Fame and Its Challenges

Christina Applegate had to deal with the challenges of celebrity that frequently come with having a great career in the entertainment business as she evolved from a teenager to an adult star. Her portrayal of Kelly Bundy in "Married with Children" thrust her into the public eye. Still, the sudden exposure also brought a host of difficulties that put her adaptation and tenacity to the test.

The public and media began to scrutinize her more as she became well-known. Christina soon discovered that being a celebrity frequently meant that everyone was watching whatever she did. Reporters would track her every step, and rumors about her personal life would often surface. The constant scrutiny produced a pressure-cooker atmosphere that made it harder and harder to maintain privacy. Christina's story served as an example of the tightrope prominent personalities have to tread while disclosing personal information and maintaining privacy.

The effect that celebrity had on Christina's mental health was one of the biggest obstacles she had to overcome. Being in the spotlight can come with much strain, and Christina was no different. She was honest about her struggles with the high expectations put on her and women in Hollywood. She struggled with low self-esteem as a result of frequent comparisons to other actors and the pressure to live up to an idealized image, which fuelled a profound sense of uneasiness and anxiety.

Christina went through a really difficult time in her life at the beginning of the new millennium. After "Married with Children" ended, she tried to reinvent herself as an actress and escape the limitations of her former part. The changeover had its challenges, though. After years of playing a role that people connected with, she felt pressure to prove she was more than just Kelly Bundy. She struggled to let go of that identity and deal with the industry's expectations at the same time.

In an attempt to change the direction of her career, Christina looked for varied parts that would highlight her range as an actress. In films like "The Sweetest Thing" and "Anchorman: The Legend of Ron Burgundy," she portrayed more mature and nuanced personas, showcasing her versatility as a comic. This development was crucial to her progress but also presented a problem: persuading people that she could go from being a sitcom star to a varied actor while still maintaining her appeal to industry insiders.

Christina also experienced severe personal difficulties during this time. Her diagnosis of breast cancer in 2008 changed her life and made her face the demands of celebrity while also considering her health and well-being. Christina found this diagnosis especially difficult to accept because she had been battling body image problems for years, made worse by the pressures of the entertainment industry. Her priorities and way of living were forced to be reevaluated as a result of the diagnosis and the treatment that followed.

She discovered that vulnerability gave her power during her cancer battle. She decided to be transparent about her journey, giving the world access to her experiences via social media and interviews. By doing this, she not only made conversations about breast cancer less stigmatizing but also strengthened her bond with her followers. Many people found great inspiration in Christina's desire to be open and honest about her struggles, and she was greatly respected for her bravery and tenacity.

Christina reinvented her personal and professional lives after overcoming her health struggle. She seized the chance to raise cancer awareness and got engaged with groups promoting breast cancer education and research. This dedication to leveraging her position for a higher good changed the perception of her celebrity. Christina positioned herself as a strong proponent of health and wellness, encouraging others to face their difficulties rather than letting her prior responsibilities define her.

CHAPTER 3: THE TRANSITION TO FILM

From Television to the Big Screen

Christina Applegate's resolve to broaden her views and push herself artistically has been a defining characteristic of her acting career in films and television. Despite becoming well-known due to her portrayal of Kelly Bundy in "Married with Children," she aimed to expand her professional horizons and demonstrate her adaptability outside television. She started this shift in the late 1990s and carried on through the new millennium, navigating the frequently challenging landscape of Hollywood's film industry.

After "Married with Children" ended in 1997, Christina had to deal with the problem of letting go of her TV persona while still trying to establish herself as a unique character in films. She played her first notable role in the

1998 comedy "The Sweetest Thing," costarring Cameron Diaz and Selma Blair. Christina showcased her development as an actress, comedic timing, and ability to deal with more mature subjects in the film. Despite receiving a mixed reception, Christina's performance was highly appreciated, and the movie eventually developed a cult following.

Christina pursued a wider variety of parts in films because of the popularity of "The Sweetest Thing." Costarring with Will Ferrell, Paul Rudd, and Steve Carell in the satirical comedy "Anchorman: The Legend of Ron Burgundy," she was directed by Adam McKay in 2004. Christina portrayed television news anchor Veronica Corningstone in this movie, trying to make it in a field that men controlled. Her performance was praised for its ability to combine strength and humor, and the movie became a cultural phenomenon with a devoted following. Christina's reputation as a gifted actress in the film business was further cemented by her ability to balance comedy and a vital female role, which struck a chord with viewers.

Following her triumph in "Anchorman," Christina continued to take on numerous roles that displayed her range. She had leading roles in films including "The Family Stone" (2005), about a young lady negotiating the complexities of her family around the holidays, and "Alvin and the Chipmunks" (2007), in which she had a supporting role. She proved her versatility as an actress in these parts by showcasing her ability to switch from comedic to more emotional and tragic performances.

But making the switch from television to film wasn't without difficulties. Christina faced the stereotypes and typecasting that come with being a television actor. Industry insiders doubted her capacity to succeed in feature films, and there were times when she wondered if she could leave her sitcom origins behind. Christina was motivated to grow as an actress and broaden her repertory, so she committed to polishing her art through various acting seminars and workshops to overcome these challenges.

Christina pursued opportunities on television that allowed her to experiment with other genres in addition to her work in films. In the highly regarded cable series "Up All Night" (2011–2012), she portrayed a newlywed mother balancing the responsibilities of her profession and family. The series displayed her humorous skills and provided a novel viewpoint on contemporary parenting. Despite its brief run, the show garnered favorable reviews and proved Christina's ongoing significance.

She took on a role in 2019 that would once again completely transform her career. She co starred with Linda Cardellini in the Netflix series "Dead to Me," a dark comedy-drama. The show's exploration of betrayal, friendship, and grief in a more severe setting allowed Christina to highlight her range as an actor. She received critical acclaim and multiple award nominations for her portrayal of widow Jen Harding, who navigates the intricacies of friendship and grief. She was nominated for a Primetime Emmy for Outstanding Lead Actress in a Comedy Series. This performance represented a significant turning point in her career and demonstrated her skill at striking the right mix between comedy and drama.

Christina Applegate's career, which has spanned from television to movies and back again, has continuously showcased her versatility in acting. She has made a name for herself in Hollywood by accepting new challenges and taking on various roles, allowing her to evolve as an artist and defy expectations. She has earned recognition in the entertainment world thanks to her dedication to her work and willingness to take risks.

Key Roles and Career Highlights

Christina Applegate's acting career is a stunning tapestry of varied parts showcasing her skill, adaptability, and tenacity. From her well-known depiction of Kelly Bundy in "Married... with Children" to her highly regarded roles in television and films, Applegate's body of work demonstrates her dedication to developing as an artist while overcoming the obstacles in the entertainment business.

Naturally, Applegate's portrayal of Kelly Bundy in "Married with Children" was one of her most important performances. After its 1987 premiere and 11 seasons, the program made Christina a well-known figure. Her hilarious and provocative portrayal of the stereotypical "dumb blonde" allowed her to challenge preconceptions while giving viewers a memorable character. Christina's reputation as a rising star in Hollywood was cemented by the several award nominations she received for this performance, including several Primetime Emmy nominations.

After "Married with Children" became successful, Christina wanted to try new things and take on more complex parts. In 1998, she starred with Cameron Diaz and Selma Blair in the romantic comedy The Sweetest Thing, which featured her comedic abilities. Despite receiving mixed reviews, Christina's portrayal was hailed for its warmth and relatability, and the movie eventually became a cult favorite.

Christina appeared in the ensemble cast of the 2004 comedy Anchorman: The Legend of Ron Burgundy, which went on to become a cultural icon. Christina played Veronica Corningstone, a persistent news anchor navigating the male-dominated broadcast industry. Because of the movie's success and exceptional performance, she gained interest from a new audience. The role gained notoriety, and many saw Christina's skill in using humor with a powerful female presence.

A significant turning point in Christina's career was her performance in "Dead to Me," which debuted in 2019 on Netflix. Christina, who co-starred alongside Linda Cardellini as widow Jen Harding, befriends Judy, a person with secrets, unexpectedly. Christina was allowed to display her dramatic range and humorous timing as the piece tackled issues of betrayal, friendship, and grief. Christina's performance in the series garnered her two nominations for a Primetime Emmy for Outstanding

Lead Actress in a Comedy Series, and the critics praised the show turned into a huge smash for Netflix, solidifying Christina's place as one of the top actresses in the business.

Christina has voiced several animated productions in addition to her well-known television and movie performances. In addition to providing the voice of "Megara" in Disney's animated feature "Hercules" (1997), she has voiced characters in other shows like "The Simpsons" and "Family Guy." Her work with animation is another evidence of her adaptability and capacity to engage people in various media.

She has also made cameos on several television programs during her career, displaying her comedic ability and openness to trying out new genres. She appeared in "Friends" as Jennifer Aniston's (Rachel's) high school rival, demonstrating her ability to fit in and leave her imprint while appearing in already popular shows.

Christina's commitment to increasing breast cancer awareness is perhaps another noteworthy aspect of her career. She became a champion for cancer research and education after receiving her diagnosis in 2008, and she used her platform to educate and motivate others going through similar struggles. In addition to inspiring many, her openness about her ordeal and the double mastectomy that followed demonstrated her dedication to vulnerability and sincerity in both her personal and professional spheres.

CHAPTER 4: EMBRACING CHANGE

Exploring New Genres: Drama and Adventure

Christina Applegate's versatility in the entertainment industry has been evident throughout her career as she has transitioned from humorous roles to more daring and tragic ones. Because of her ability to venture outside her comfort zone, she has demonstrated her versatility as an actress. She interacts with various stories that appeal to audiences of different demographics.

She made a noteworthy dramatic debut in the television movie "The Dead Will Tell" (2004), playing a lady who gets entangled in a murder case involving her fiancé. With this part, Christina left her humorous history behind and showed off her ability to handle the intricacies of a dramatic story. Critics commended her performance, pointing out that she could arouse various emotions while addressing justice, love, and grief issues.

Christina's portrayal of a dramatic woman in the Netflix series "Dead to Me" in 2019 further cemented her dramatic skills. She played Jen Harding, a recently bereaved lady navigating her grief and the difficulties of emerging connections, co-starring Linda Cardellini. Christina could delve deeply into the subtleties of her character's emotional journey thanks to the show's deft blending of poignant drama and dark comedy. She received two Primetime Emmy nominations for Outstanding Lead Actress in a Comedy Series due to the positive reviews she received for her performance. Christina's range as an actress was demonstrated by her ability to offer tragic and comic moments in a series that dealt with complex issues like betrayal, forgiveness, and grief.

She has dabbled in the adventure genre in addition to television dramas, especially with productions that combine comedy and action components. Christina played Rusty Griswold's adult wife, Debbie, alongside Ed Helms in the 2015 revival of the beloved movie series "Vacation." The Griswold family is followed throughout the movie as they go on a crazy cross-country car trip. Despite mainly being a comedy, the film also has adventure components, emphasizing Christina's versatility in toning down her comic style.

Christina extended her excursion into the genre by appearing in the 2007 film Alvin and the Chipmunks and its follow-ups. She portrayed Claire Wilson and Dave Seville's (Jason Lee) love interest in three family-friendly movies. The films showcased Christina's ability to connect with younger viewers while navigating the fast-paced, often chaotic world of the Chipmunks. Christina blended aspects of adventure, comedy, and music in these flicks.

In addition to her film career, Christina's flexibility is shown through her stage background. In the musical "Sweet Charity," she debuted on Broadway in 2005, assuming the lead role of Charity Hope Valentine. Through this experience, she explored musical theater's dramatic themes while showcasing her vocal ability. Critics praised her seamless move from television to the stage as evidence of her commitment to expanding her creative horizons.

Christina Applegate has always embraced different genres in cinema and television throughout her career. Because of her willingness to seek drama and adventure, she has been able to challenge herself as an actress and establish a stronger connection with audiences. She has made a name for herself as an adaptable performer who can connect with intricate characters and narratives by assuming a variety of parts that cross genres.

Collaborations with Renowned Directors

Christina Applegate has collaborated with several renowned filmmakers over her career, which has helped her advance as an actress and artist. These partnerships have produced standout performances highlighting her range and nuance as a performer. Her career has been greatly influenced by her desire to take on various parts under the direction of different directors.

Director "James Burrows" was one of Christina's first notable partners when she worked on "Married with Children" Burrows, a renowned director well known for his work on several sitcoms, contributed to creating the distinct humorous tone of the program, which Christina used to hone her comedic timing and flesh out her role of Kelly Bundy. This partnership significantly shaped her career, as the show became well-known, making her a well-known humorous actor.

Christina worked with director Peter Segal in the romantic comedy "The Sweetest Thing" (2002) to broaden her career beyond sitcoms. Christina acted with Cameron Diaz and Selma Blair in this movie, and Segal's direction allowed her to explore a more humorous and daring side of her persona. The romantic and humorous elements of the film gave Christina a chance to show off her comedy skills, and Segal's skill at directing ensemble casts enhanced the movie's overall appeal.

She worked with filmmaker Adam McKay on "Anchorman: The Legend of Ron Burgundy" (2004); this partnership would turn out to be a turning point in Christina's career. Christina excelled as Veronica Corningstone, a strong-willed news anchor in a newsroom dominated by men, thanks to McKay's distinct humorous vision. The movie became a cultural icon, and Christina's performance won her critical praise, further cementing her place as one of Hollywood's top actresses. The movie's popularity was mainly due to the chemistry between the actors, which was enhanced by McKay's collaborative directing style.

Christina's partnership with director Greg Berlanti in the television series "Dead to Me" (2019) was another significant one. Berlanti, renowned for his work on several hit television shows, gave the dark comedy-drama a new angle. Under his direction, Christina explored the depths of her character, Jen Harding, as she dealt with betrayal, friendship, and grief. Christina and the series received critical acclaim, including two Emmy nominations for Christina's performance, thanks to Berlanti's direction of the show's inventive storyline and excellent character development.

She has collaborated with directors, including Drew Barrymore and Jenna Bans. Her role in Barrymore's 2009 film Whip It signaled Christina's serious entry into a more dramatic role. Under Barrymore's supervision, Christina was able to demonstrate her development as an actress and explore a range of complicated emotions in her role. Similarly, Christina and Jenna Bans worked closely together as writers and producers on "Dead to Me," influencing Christina's performance and plot.

Christina Applegate has worked with a wide range of well-known filmmakers over her career, and each of them has impacted her development as an actress. These partnerships have allowed Christina to demonstrate her versatility and adjust to different directing styles, from her early sitcom work to her recent dramatic roles. Each collaboration has aided her development as an actress, allowing her to traverse several genres successfully and provide spectators with unforgettable performances.

CHAPTER 5: PERSONAL STRUGGLES

Battling Personal Challenges and Health Issues

Christina Applegate has faced her fair share of personal hardships and health problems throughout her career in Hollywood. Despite her successful profession, the major challenges she has experienced have tested her tenacity and strength. In addition to molding her character, her capacity to overcome these obstacles has strengthened her bond with her audience, who respect her bravery and vulnerability in the face of difficulty.

The 2008 diagnosis of Christina's breast cancer was one of the most significant turning points in her life. She was only thirty-six years old at the time. Her family and supporters were as shocked by the prognosis as she was.

Christina decided to get a double mastectomy as a symbol of her will to take charge of her health and destiny. She has discussed in interviews the emotional torment she went through at this time, battling fears of losing her femininity and the disease's effects on her life and profession.

Christina became a vocal supporter of breast cancer research and awareness after her surgery. She made the most of her position to inform people about the value of early detection and the realities of having cancer. Her triumphant announcement in 2012 that she was cancer-free struck a profound chord with her followers. Christina's candidness regarding her struggle with breast cancer de-stigmatized the illness and motivated numerous women to confront comparable obstacles. She developed into an advocate for female emancipation, stressing the value of frequent screenings and self-evaluation.

She has experienced other personal difficulties in addition to her cancer diagnosis. She disclosed in 2021 that she had multiple sclerosis (MS), a degenerative condition affecting the central nervous system. The news took many people aback, and Christina openly discussed the challenges she had managing the illness while continuing her career in entertainment. Despite experiencing increased fatigue and difficulty moving about as a result of her diagnosis, Christina stayed dedicated to her work and her advocacy for people with chronic illnesses.

Christina's outlook on life has been dramatically impacted by her experiences with MS and breast cancer. She has discussed in interviews how her priorities and relationships have changed as a result of these health issues, which has led her to adopt a more balanced approach to her personal and professional lives. She has stressed the value of mental health and self-care and has pushed people to put their needs ahead of society's.

She has depended on her friends and family throughout these trying times. Her close-knit relationships have given her a solid base to balance the intricacies of her health. Sadie Grace, Christina's 2011 daughter, has also greatly impacted her life by encouraging and cheering her up when things become challenging. Christina has talked a lot about how becoming a mother has changed her perspective and made her see how important it is to be strong and resilient.

Christina Applegate has demonstrated incredible bravery and tenacity in the face of adversity. Many others have found resonance in her ability to address personal health difficulties head-on, turning her struggles into chances for advocacy and awareness. By telling her tale, Christina encourages others and strengthens the bonds between those going through comparable struggles. Her story is a powerful example for many people facing similar obstacles, highlighting the value of empathy, understanding, and the ability to be vulnerable in the face of hardship.

The Importance of Support Systems

Christina Applegate has continuously stressed the need for support networks to overcome obstacles in her personal and professional life and career. Her struggles with health concerns and her early days in the entertainment industry have all shown how important it is to have the support of friends, family, and coworkers to overcome hardship, build resilience, and succeed in her job.

Her network of support has always revolved around her family. She frequently discusses her close bond with her parents, especially actress and singer Nancy Priddy. Christina was encouraged to pursue her love of performing at a young age because she grew up in a creative family. Her mother's mentoring during her formative years helped shape her understanding of the entertainment world. Christina's parents have encouraged her during different stages of her life and provided a secure environment in which she may communicate her goals and anxieties.

Christina is a mother who recognizes the value of strong family ties. She frequently talks about how her 2011-born daughter, Sadie Grace, has become a significant source of strength and happiness. Because of her experiences as a parent, Christina has a deeper appreciation for the support of her family. This has enabled her to both provide a loving environment for Sadie and rely on them for help when she needs it—particularly during her struggles with multiple sclerosis and cancer.

Her career and friendship contacts have greatly augmented Christina's support network and her family. Being in the entertainment business may be difficult, but finding friends and coworkers aware of celebrity demands can be a comforting emotional support system. Many of her co-stars, including "Linda Cardellini" from "Dead to Me" and "Cameron Diaz" from "The Sweetest Thing," are still friends with Christina. These connections have given her a sense of community, enabling her to talk about her experiences and get guidance from people who have gone through comparable obstacles in their professional lives.

The cast members' sociability on set can also foster an encouraging atmosphere. Christina has talked about the supportive environment that existed on the "Dead to Me" set because of the cast and crew's cooperation and respect for one another. Thanks to the group's support, Christina was able to manage her health issues and the emotional demands of her character.

Christina is an advocate for raising awareness and providing support for people dealing with comparable health challenges as a result of her experiences with multiple sclerosis and breast cancer. She has inspired people to get help and expand their support systems by using her platform. Many people have been motivated to talk about their troubles by Christina's honesty, which has helped to create a sense of support among individuals dealing with comparable health issues.

In interviews, she has emphasized the value of getting help from therapists, support groups, and medical specialists. Christina has shown how important it is to have a solid support network when managing chronic conditions. By sharing her story, she has inspired people to prioritize their health and well-being while seeking support from their loved ones.

Christina Applegate's experience emphasizes how vital vulnerability is to building genuine connections. By being transparent about her challenges, she has developed a network of supporters and admirers who can relate to her experience and receive assistance from her family and friends. Her readiness to open up about her experiences reminds us that showing vulnerability to others can strengthen our relationships with them and garner their support.

In the end, Christina's tale emphasizes how crucial support networks are for overcoming obstacles in life. These connections—whether made via family, friends, or community activism—offer a safety net during trying times and help people find resiliency, hope, and strength. Christina Applegate's stories provide compelling evidence that we are never alone in our challenges and that, with the right help, we can overcome any obstacle in our path.

CHAPTER 6: A NEW CHAPTER

Becoming a Mother: Balancing Career and Family

Her path into motherhood has profoundly impacted Christina Applegate's life and work. Christina gave birth to her daughter Sadie Grace on January 27, 2011, and she has talked extensively about the pleasures and difficulties of juggling her busy career in the entertainment business with her role as a working mother. Her approach to her personal and professional endeavors was impacted by this transformation's new insights and priorities.

After years of negotiating Hollywood's matrimonial maze, Christina declared her desire for a child. She has stated in interviews that having a child and realizing the value of a family result from her business experiences. Christina's life took a significant turn when she and her then-fiance, Martyn LeNoble, welcomed their daughter Sadie into it. She has frequently talked about how much love she experienced when she became a parent, calling it one of the most amazing experiences of her life.

Christina faced particular difficulties in juggling the obligations of motherhood with the demands of a prosperous acting career. Her job schedule had to be adjusted frequently to accommodate her daughter's requirements, especially in the early years when Sadie was still a toddler. Christina has admitted that it was challenging to strike this balance, particularly in light of how erratic the entertainment business can be. However, she prioritized being there for her kid, proving her dedication to her family.

She has been transparent about her desire to be a devoted mother, highlighting how becoming a mother has changed her perspective and allowed her to reframe what success means. She has stated in interviews that she frequently chooses roles that will enable her to spend time with Sadie, demonstrating her dedication to upholding a close family relationship while pursuing her acting career. Her readiness to put her family above her career has been shown by her refusal to accept assignments that would need her to spend a lot of time away from home. This is a result of her dedication to motherhood.

Christina has found that her family and friends' support has been invaluable in juggling parenthood and her profession. She has talked kindly about the practical and emotional support her mother and her close friends gave her during her parenting adventure. Thanks to this support system, she has efficiently organized her time, enabling her to actively participate in Sadie's life and perform her obligations at work.

Furthermore, Christina and Martyn LeNoble's collaboration has been essential to their shared parenting duties. The pair has strongly emphasized working together to raise their daughter, frequently working together to provide Sadie with a secure and loving home. They have been able to support one another in striking a balance between work and family life by having a mutual knowledge of each other's occupations, which has strengthened the basis for their family.

Christina's notion of success changed as she adapted to being a mother. Although her career is still essential to her, becoming a mother brings her more joy and fulfillment than any job she has ever had. She can now prioritize initiatives that support her principles and enable her to maintain a healthy work-life balance, which has changed how she approaches her profession.

Christina has advocated for working parents to take care of themselves in addition to their duty as mothers. She stresses the importance of prioritizing mental and emotional health and encourages other mothers to get help and make time for themselves. By being upfront and honest about her experiences, Christina has demonstrated the value of promoting a supportive community among parents by talking honestly about the difficulties of motherhood.

Ultimately, Christina Applegate's path to motherhood has molded her identity and impacted how she approaches her work and life. Christina has faced difficulties juggling her obligations as a mother and an actress, but her dedication to them has helped her build a happy and purposeful life. Her story speaks to many working parents who try to strike a balance between their personal and professional lives, showing that it's okay to follow one's ambitions and enjoy motherhood at the same time.

Finding Strength in Vulnerability

Many instances in Christina Applegate's life and career highlight the tremendous power of vulnerability. In addition to fostering connections with others, her willingness to be transparent about her difficulties and problems has shown that owning up to one's shortcomings can be a source of strength. Christina's journey has been shaped by her acceptance of vulnerability as a fundamental aspect of who she is and how she experiences both her personal and professional life.

Christina has been faithful to who she is since the beginning of her career. She has shown the value of staying true to oneself, whether it is through her on-screen personas or her public disclosures of personal details. When she started talking about her struggles with health difficulties, such as her 2008 breast cancer diagnosis and her subsequent 2021 multiple sclerosis (MS) diagnosis, her honesty was even more evident. By being open and honest about her health issues, Christina has inspired others to accept their weaknesses and brought attention to these conditions. She has stated in interviews that while facing the dread and uncertainty that came with her diagnosis was intimidating, doing so eventually resulted in personal development. Because so many people can relate to Christina's experiences of sorrow, fear, and resiliency, her honesty has helped her audience feel more connected to her.

Christina is now an enthusiastic supporter of health awareness due to her experiences with MS and breast cancer. She was involved in several campaigns to encourage breast cancer screening and research after receiving a diagnosis of the disease. Christina has been transparent about her experience, talking about the value of early identification and the psychological effects of cancer therapy. Her readiness to be vulnerable with others has given them the confidence to put their health first and ask for help when needed. Christina has also utilized her platform to dispel myths and raise awareness of multiple sclerosis, emphasizing the difficulties associated with the illness. She has aided in humanizing these health challenges by revealing her struggles and inspiring empathy and compassion among her audience. Her advocacy work is a testament to the power of vulnerability, as she uses her experiences to inform essential outreach initiatives.

Christina believes that being strong entails acknowledging and embracing one's weaknesses in addition to tenacity. She has talked about how her experiences with health issues have changed her perception of what it means to be strong in interviews. Christina uses her vulnerability as a source of power rather than seeing it as a weakness. She emphasizes that sharing one's experiences can foster healing and a sense of connection, enabling people to assist one another through shared hardships. Her artwork reflects this way of thinking. In the Netflix series "Dead to Me," Christina played a lady who was experiencing loss and sadness. Because of the role's emotional depth, which connected to her own experiences, she was able to explore her vulnerabilities as an actress. This honest portrayal of complex emotions and her performance's enrichment demonstrated to the audience how storytelling can be enhanced by accepting vulnerability.

Her story has also brought attention to how crucial community is for people who need it to discover strength in vulnerability. She has talked extensively about the relationships she has built throughout her life, from her family to her close friends and coworkers, all of whom have been supportive. These relationships have given her a secure platform to communicate her worries and fears, confirming that vulnerability flourishes in a compassionate and understanding atmosphere. Through her advocacy work, Christina has helped people with MS and breast cancer feel more connected to one another. She promotes candid discussions about health issues, giving people a platform to support one another and exchange personal stories. This community-based approach highlights the power of vulnerability to unite individuals and form ties that promote resilience and healing.

By accepting her vulnerabilities, Christina Applegate has shown that vulnerability and openness to one's challenges are the keys to strength. Her experience has shown how crucial community, activism, and sincerity are to overcoming obstacles in life. By being transparent about her health problems, she has encouraged people to accept their frailties and created a supportive and understanding environment.

CHAPTER 7: ADVOCACY AND AWARENESS

Raising Awareness for Breast Cancer

Christina Applegate's experience with breast cancer has had a significant impact on both her life and her dedication to spreading awareness of the illness. Christina was 36 years old when she received her breast cancer diagnosis in 2008 following a standard mammography. It surprised her even more when the diagnosis was made because her mother, Nancy, had survived breast cancer, and her aunt had also suffered from the condition. Christina was inspired to take against breast cancer head-on by her connection to the illness.

She made the proactive decision to have a double mastectomy after learning of her illness. She has been transparent about her decision to have this surgery, stating that it was a decision that would save her life. She has said in interviews that the surgery was a challenging but necessary step and that she is appreciative of the advancements in medical technology that have made it possible for her to make well-informed decisions regarding her health. Many people have found that Christina's openness about her personal experience with breast cancer has helped to demystify the illness and motivate others to prioritize their health and get regular checkups.

Christina developed a strong interest in raising awareness of breast cancer after receiving her diagnosis and undergoing treatment. She eagerly took part in several public awareness programs and activities that sought to inform people about the value of early detection and the support available to individuals impacted by breast cancer. Christina has made use of her famous status to raise awareness of the mental and physical difficulties associated with having breast cancer and to illuminate the reality of living with the disease. To lessen stigma and encourage women to take preventative health steps, she has promoted candid conversations about breast health.

She is one of the co-founders of the nonprofit organization Right Action for Women, which was established in 2012 to help women who are at high risk of breast cancer financially. The organization's goal is to assist people who might find it difficult to pay for preventive treatments and screenings. Christina has significantly improved the lives of numerous women through her advocacy efforts, highlighting the value of having access to support and medical care.

Furthermore, Christina's fight against breast cancer has motivated her to advocate vocally for genetic counseling and testing. Having tested positive for the BRCA1 gene mutation, which raises the risk of ovarian and breast cancers considerably, she has advised women to think about getting tested genetically and to be mindful of their family history. Thanks to Christina's openness to share her story, many others have been given the confidence to take control of their health and make knowledgeable decisions about their medical care.

Christina received the Susan G. Komen Foundation's "Advocacy Award" in 2013 to appreciate her work promoting breast cancer awareness and supporting people impacted by the disease. Many people are still moved by her job because she uses her experiences to motivate people to prioritize their health and well-being. Christina has raised awareness and funds for breast cancer awareness through her participation in fundraising events, appearances in public service announcements, and social media usage.

In addition to increasing public awareness of breast cancer, Christina Applegate's support has helped survivors and those impacted by the illness feel more connected to one another. She has emphasized the value of support networks and urged women to rely on friends, relatives, and medical experts when they travel. Her courage to be vulnerable has made it possible for people to welcome and promote candid discussions about breast cancer.

Empowering Others Through Personal Experience

Christina Applegate's breast cancer journey and her post-trauma experiences have inspired and empowered countless others going through similar struggles. Christina accepted her role as an advocate and mentor after receiving her diagnosis in 2008, utilizing her own experience to encourage and uplift others in the battle against breast cancer. Her openness about her difficulties has been essential in de-stigmatizing the illness and promoting candid discussions about health.

Following her diagnosis, Christina talked about her experience on a variety of media outlets, describing not just the physical difficulties she faced but also the psychological and emotional toll that her illness had on her. Through her open discussion of her experience, from her early doubts and anxieties to her choice to have a double mastectomy, Christina has given those who might otherwise feel alone in their struggles a voice. Her openness to sharing such personal information has made breast cancer survivors and those impacted by the disease feel more understood and supported.

Christina strongly emphasizes the value of early detection and preventative health interventions, which is a noteworthy component of her advocacy. She has often urged women to put their health first by making routine mammogram appointments and having candid discussions about personal risks and family histories with their healthcare providers. Christina has inspired others to take control of their health by sharing her story of early detection and her choice to get tested genetically. She has also emphasized the importance of education as a potent weapon in the battle against cancer.

She has actively participated in support groups and projects geared at empowering women who have breast cancer, in addition to her work as a public advocate. She has reached a wider audience through participating in organizations like the Susan G. Komen Foundation and her co-founding of Right Action for Women. She has helped people navigate the complexities of their diagnoses and treatment options by offering them emotional support and financial assistance through these platforms.

Many others have found resonance in Christina's honesty, especially those who might be reluctant to talk about their health issues. By being vulnerable, she has made it safe for people to voice their worries and anxieties, which has helped them feel less alone on their journeys. Her honesty has also encouraged others to tell their tales, strengthening the bond between survivors and those receiving therapy.

Furthermore, Christina's dedication to uplifting people goes beyond the context of breast cancer. She has taken advantage of her position to promote mental health awareness, especially when it comes to managing a chronic condition. Acknowledging that cancer can have a significant emotional impact, she has urged people to prioritize their mental health and seek assistance. Christina's support of mental health has brought attention to how crucial it is to deal with the psychological effects of medical issues, enabling people to seek holistic ways to their treatment.

Christina Applegate spreads the word about embracing one's journey via social media interactions, public appearances, and countless interviews. For many, her bravery and tenacity in overcoming her health issues are a source of inspiration. Christina is a prime example of the power of sharing one's experience and its ability to raise awareness, encourage support, and inspire change. She did this by turning her problems into inspiration for others.

Christina's story shows how meaningful advocacy may be fuelled by personal experiences that empower others. Using her struggles as a platform for awareness, she has changed her life and the lives of countless others fighting comparable struggles. Her unwavering dedication to spreading awareness and helping others on their travels exemplifies the grit and resiliency that can come from hardship, encouraging individuals to believe in their strength in the face of difficulties.

CHAPTER 8: RETURNING TO COMEDY

The Success of "Dead to Me"

Liz Feldman co-created the Netflix dark comedy series Dead to Me, which became a significant turning point in Christina Applegate's career. In the show's May 3, 2019, premiere, Christina plays Jen Harding, a recently widowed woman who befriends Judy Hale, played by Linda Cardellini. The show blends humor with moving emotional scenes as it tackles topics of friendship, loss, and life's intricacies.

"Dead to Me" immediately won praise from critics for its performances, screenplay, and original storytelling technique. Christina received appreciation from reviewers and viewers alike for her portrayal of Jen, a lady struggling with her husband's unexpected death. Christina's performance demonstrated her emotional range and humorous timing. Viewers were drawn to the show because of its clever storytelling and keen wit, which developed a devoted following.

"Dead to Me" is noteworthy for examining intricate female relationships. The show delves deeply into Jen and Judy's connection, uncovering layers of emotional problems, secrets, and betrayal. The show's popularity was primarily attributed to Christina and Linda Cardellini's chemistry. Their genuine performances won praise for enabling viewers to relate to the characters on a personal level. "Dead to Me" stands apart from other television programs in its genre because of its focus on female empowerment and friendship.

Deeper issues, including mourning, mental health, and the effects of trauma, were also acknowledged in the series. Many viewers could identify with Christina's depiction of Jen's emotional challenges and journey toward healing because they could relate to the story's emotional complexity. This relatability gave the comedy on the show more nuance and a well-balanced tone that kept viewers interested.

Shortly after its premiere, "Dead to Me" was renewed for a second season due to its rapid rise to fame in popular culture and the show's increasing popularity; its second season debuted on May 8, 2020. Christina received much attention for her performance in Season 2, especially considering her health issues. She was given a multiple sclerosis diagnosis in 2021, which gave her performance of Jen more depth in real life as she dealt with comparable challenges on screen.

In the third and final season of the show, which debuted on November 17, 2022, she brought Jen and Judy's journey to a close for viewers. Christina's skill and commitment as an actress were demonstrated by her ability to balance comedy with drama, even in the middle of her struggles. Her portrayal in "Dead to Me" brought her numerous honors and nominations, including a Primetime Emmy nomination for Outstanding Lead Actress in a Comedy Series.

In addition to enhancing Christina Applegate's reputation as a talented actor, "Dead to Me"'s success created new opportunities for her career. It allowed her to work on projects that defy conventional television plots and take on more varied roles. The program's influence went beyond straightforward enjoyment; discussions about the value of mental health, the difficulties of grieving, and the resilience of female friendships were spurred.

All things considered, "Dead to Me" is a monument to Christina Applegate's fortitude and acting prowess. Her portrayal of Jen Harding struck a chord with many people, demonstrating her deft handling of both emotional and humorous components. The show has significantly impacted television history by highlighting the ability of narrative to unite people and spark discussion, as well as by highlighting Christina's long-lasting contributions to the field.

Reinventing Comedy in a New Era

Christina Applegate has been instrumental in redefining humor at a time when the television industry is undergoing significant change. The stories and humor that connected with viewers changed along with the entertainment business. This transition has been typified by Christina's work in the late 2010s, especially with programs like "Dead to Me," which combine conventional comedy aspects with deeper themes of loss, sadness, and resiliency.

The popularity of streaming services has made it possible to experiment more with comedic formats. More sophisticated storytelling that addresses current societal issues has gradually replaced traditional sitcoms, which were frequently dependent on laugh tracks and repetitive narratives. Christina's character in "Dead to Me" is a prime example of this change since the show uses dark humor to examine the intricacies of interpersonal relationships and the effects of trauma.

Audiences looking for relatability and sincerity in their entertainment find great resonance with this approach.

In "Dead to Me," Christina plays Jen Harding, a contemporary lady coping with significant obstacles in life. The show frequently combines humorous situations with somber themes like betrayal and bereavement, giving rise to its humor. Comedy has never looked better thanks to this delicate balance between humor and emotional nuance, which allows viewers to connect with the characters on several levels. Christina's performance greatly aids this strategy, highlighting her talent for fusing dramatic nuance with humorous timing.

The topics covered in "Dead to Me" also mirror more significant societal shifts when discussing trauma, mental health, and female empowerment. Comedy's conventional gender stereotypes are challenged by Christina's portrayal of a woman negotiating the intricacies of friendship and widowhood. Stories that speak to a wide range of audiences can now be told because it gives a more realistic portrayal of women's experiences. Christina contributes to deconstructing the frequently shallow representation of women in humorous roles by embracing sensitivity and sincerity in her persona.

In addition, Christina Applegate's support of mental health awareness has influenced her comic endeavors. Since learning that she had multiple sclerosis in 2021, she has advocated for compassion and empathy for others who are going through similar struggles by using her platform. Her humorous parts gain depth from this real-life experience, enabling her to establish a personal connection with the audience. Her readiness to open up about her experience indicates a movement in contemporary comedy that values openness and honesty, which helps create a more inclusive story environment.

Christina is part of a generation of comedians who are changing the genre; therefore, her effect goes beyond individual performances. Her work is an excellent example of how humor can be a potent weapon for confronting complex emotional themes, particularly when the lines between comedy and drama become blurry. The popularity of programs like "Dead to Me" has made room for more varied humor storytelling, bringing in fresh voices and viewpoints.

CHAPTER 9: LIFE BEYOND ACTING

Business Ventures and Production Work

Christina Applegate's career is not limited to acting; she has also made successful forays into production and business, showcasing her diverse skill set and sharp sense of entrepreneurship. These endeavors demonstrate her ability to traverse the complexity of Hollywood while empowering herself and others, and they demonstrate her awareness of the entertainment industry from both a creative and a business standpoint.

Christina founded "Green Eggs and Ham Productions," a production company, as one of her noteworthy business endeavors to take charge of her career and produce material that aligns with her moral principles. Christina's transition into producing enables her to pursue her passions for curating and developing projects in addition to acting, guaranteeing that the tales being portrayed are true to her vision and experiences. Her love for telling more complex and varied stories—especially ones that emphasize women's perspectives—also drives her ambition to create content.

She has worked as an executive producer on several projects in addition to her work; the most notable is the critically praised television series "Dead to Me." The 2019 Netflix original dark comedy marked a significant turning point in her career. As an executive producer, Christina helped steer the show on the right path and preserve its distinct style of heartfelt storytelling mixed with humor. The show's success enhanced her standing as a shrewd operator in the entertainment sector.

Christina has also dabbled in product endorsements and branding. She has participated in several ads and companies, associating herself with goods consistent with her interests and values. Her work with companies such as Sofia Vergara's apparel line for Kmart demonstrates her ability to find collaborations that appeal to her target market. Christina has always had a picky approach to brand endorsements; she likes to collaborate with companies that genuinely resonate with her and represent who she is.

Furthermore, Christina Applegate has used her business endeavors to further her charitable efforts. She has collaborated with groups that promote breast cancer education and research, using her position to speak out in favor of worthy causes. Her capacity to use her notoriety for charitable causes demonstrates her dedication to changing the world, especially in fields that are meaningful to her. This fits with her story of activism and resiliency since she freely discusses her experiences to encourage and elevate those going through comparable struggles.

Christina's work progression showcases her flexibility and foresight. As the entertainment industry changes, she has embraced new opportunities and technologies, such as the emergence of streaming platforms, to reach a larger audience for her work. Christina's ability to switch from acting to producing and running her own company demonstrates her grasp of the business's workings and her will to stay current.

Philanthropy and Giving Back

Christina Applegate has long been well-known for her charitable work. She uses her influence and life experiences to promote and encourage support for various organizations. She has been actively involved in philanthropic endeavors her entire career, especially those that raise awareness of breast cancer and other health and women's issues.

She has contributed significantly to breast cancer research and awareness as part of her charitable endeavors. Following a double mastectomy due to her personal experience with breast cancer in 2008, Christina became a vocal supporter of early diagnosis and the value of testing for health issues. Her fight with cancer inspired her dedication to supporting those who might have the same difficulties. Christina has been involved in several initiatives to educate women about breast cancer and their options. Her honesty in her diagnosis and course of treatment has aided in de-stigmatizing the discussion of breast cancer and inspired innumerable women to place a high priority on their health.

Christina established the nonprofit "Right Action for Women" foundation in 2010 to help women who are at high risk of breast cancer financially. The charity wants to make potentially life-saving exams and preventative actions more accessible to women, especially those who might not have the financial means to do so. Christina has made tremendous progress in enabling women to take control of their health and seek early intervention through her campaign. The group emphasizes the value of making educated decisions about one's health and also works to increase public knowledge of genetic testing for breast cancer.

She is a philanthropist who goes above and beyond raising awareness of breast cancer. She has participated in a number of groups that assist struggling families and women. For example, she has contributed to St. Jude Children's Research Hospital, which treats children with cancer and other serious illnesses. Christina's involvement in St. Jude fundraising events demonstrates her commitment to enhancing the lives of marginalized groups and advancing vital research on diseases affecting children.

Christina is not only involved with charities that support health, but she has also supported animal rights concerns. She has participated in campaigns encouraging adoption and ethical pet ownership and advocates for animal welfare organizations. Christina's activism, which aims to increase public understanding of the value of treating animals with respect and compassion, clearly reflects her love for animals.

Christina Applegate has motivated others to participate in humanitarian endeavors and brought essential health issues to the public's attention through her philanthropic activity. She has encouraged her fans and followers to get engaged and give back to their communities by using her celebrity status to draw attention to problems that are important to her. Christina has profoundly influenced many people's lives by sharing her personal story and utilizing her platform to push for change.

Furthermore, Christina's generosity reflects her faith in the strength of support and community. She frequently stresses the value of uniting to support people in need and cultivating an attitude of empathy and compassion. This philosophy is evident in her philanthropic work, as she tries to provide a haven for people going through trying times.

CHAPTER 10: LEGACY AND INFLUENCE

Christina's Impact on Comedy and Culture

Christina Applegate's varied performances, unique comic style, and contributions to television and movies have made an enduring impression on the comedy world and popular culture. An actress renowned for fusing humor and poignant moments, Christina has influenced comedy and connected with audiences of all ages.

Her legendary performance as Kelly Bundy on the popular sitcom "Married with Children," which ran from 1987 to 1997, marked the beginning of her ascent to fame. Christina's portrayal of Al and Peggy Bundy's flashy and frequently naive daughter went viral. The program defied social conventions and stretched the bounds of conventional family representations, setting new standards for television humor. Christina's portrayal was a significant factor in the show's popularity since her character's outrageous actions and catchy one-liners enthralled audiences and had a big impression on pop culture. Kelly Bundy typified the 1990s comedy era, and Christina's ability to deliver intelligent comedic timing contributed to the series' iconic popularity.

Following "Married with Children," Christina worked on several projects that significantly advanced the comedy subgenre. Her role as Rachel Green's college flatmate, Amy Green, in the highly acclaimed television series "Friends" demonstrated her ability to hold her own with an impressive ensemble cast. Her breadth and ability were showcased by her guest appearances on such a popular series, which further cemented her image as a comedic artist.

Christina was successful in the 2000s when she starred in her television series, "Samantha Who?" in which she portrayed Samantha Newly, a lady with amnesia who must find her identity and life. Positive reviews were received for the program, which showcased Christina's ability to tackle more profound issues of personal growth and self-discovery alongside comedy. She was nominated for multiple awards for her work, including Outstanding Lead Actress in a Comedy Series for the Emmy Award. Christina demonstrated her development as an actress and her ability to change with the times with her work on "Samantha Who?"

Christina's turn in the dark comedy series "Dead to Me," which debuted on Netflix in 2019, was one of her most considerable contributions to modern comedy. Christina plays the role of "Jen Harding" in the show, a widow who befriends Judy Hale, portrayed by Linda Cardellini, unexpectedly. Christina gained praise from critics for her performance, which deftly combines humor with touching themes of friendship, forgiveness, and loss in this series. "Dead to Me" redefined the bar for female-led comedies by examining intricate female relationships and willingness to inject humor into weighty issues. Christina's depiction of Jen demonstrated the breadth of her skill as she brought humor and genuineness to the part while navigating a spectrum of emotions. The show's popularity strengthened Christina's position as a major force in comedy.

Beyond her stand-alone roles, Christina Applegate has been instrumental in changing the perception of women in comedy. Her characters frequently dispel clichés and offer complex portraits of women overcoming obstacles in their personal and professional lives. Christina has paved the way for upcoming female comedians and actors by bringing relatability and sincerity to her performances. Because of her success, women are now more frequently represented in humorous roles that showcase their strengths and complexities more inclusively and diversely.

Christina has made significant contributions to television, but her influence on comedic films is equally essential. Among the well-known films in which she has acted are "The Sweetest Thing" and "Anchorman: The Legend of Ron Burgundy." She played the legendary role of "Veronica Corningstone" in "Anchorman," a newsroom dominated by men, and she portrayed a strong, ambitious female journalist. The movie itself went on to become a cultural icon, and Christina's performance contributed to a new definition of female comedic roles by portraying them as strong, independent women rather than sticking to clichés.

Her impact goes beyond her stage appearances; she has actively created works of fiction and poetry that showcase her sense of humor. By taking charge of her stories, she has supported narratives that speak to her experiences, allowing her to have various effects on the comedy genre.

Christina Applegate has had a profound and wide-ranging influence on humor and culture. Her reputation as a critical player in the entertainment industry has been cemented by her ability to combine humor with poignant moments, her dedication to accurate representations of women, and her willingness to tackle complex subjects. Christina inspires audiences and fellow artists, creating a generation-spanning legacy of humor, resiliency, and empowerment. Christina remains a creative and inspirational figure in the rapidly changing comedy and popular culture worlds despite juggling her personal and professional obligations.

Inspiration for Future Generations

Future generations can draw inspiration from Christina Applegate's experience in the entertainment industry, which exemplifies skill, perseverance, and the value of authenticity. As a versatile actress, she has negotiated both personal and professional obstacles, constantly pushing the envelope and supporting worthy causes. Many aspiring actors, actresses, and anyone trying to carve out their paths in a world that frequently restricts them can relate to her experience.

Christina has been a prime example of the value of adaptability in the entertainment business, from her early days on "Married... with Children" to her recent triumph in "Dead to Me." Her ability to switch between humor and drama demonstrates her commitment to her art and inspires aspiring actors to experiment with many genres and techniques. Christina has frequently underlined the importance of developing one's abilities and not being afraid of obstacles. She is a reminder that hard work and dedication, rather than just receiving recognition, truly characterize success.

Her reputation as an inspiration has been further established by her openness regarding her problems, especially her fight with breast cancer. Following her 2017 diagnosis, she shared her experiences to aid others and turned into an advocate for early detection and breast cancer awareness. Christina's openness about her health experience has encouraged others going through similar struggles by motivating them to get help and put their health first. Her bravery in speaking up about these problems shows the value of vulnerability and how it may build relationships and hope.

Christina inspires future generations with her dedication to being a working mother in the entertainment world and her advocacy efforts. She has successfully juggled the demands of her busy work with her motherhood, frequently discussing the pleasures and difficulties of parenthood in interviews. Christina has inspired young women to embrace their personal and professional goals by demonstrating that it is possible to follow one's dreams and raise a family. Her experiences demonstrate the value of self-care, support networks, and setting priorities for essential things in life.

In addition, Christina Applegate's influence on how women are portrayed in the media has created opportunities for upcoming female talent. She has constantly opted for parts that defy expectations and portray nuanced, multifaceted personalities. By doing this, she has influenced how women are depicted in films and television shows, encouraging aspiring actors to look for parts that highlight their strength and uniqueness. Christina's accomplishments in various positions show that women can lead the narrative genre, shattering stereotypes and creating more chances for upcoming female talent.

Beyond her work in acting, Christina has contributed her creativity to developing and producing projects aligned with her vision and ideals. Her behind-the-scenes work emphasizes the value of storytelling from various perspectives and gives young creators the confidence to take ownership of their narratives. Christina can shape the narratives through her production work, inspiring the next generation to find their creative voices and push for more excellent representation in the business.

Christina Applegate is a shining example of what it means to be resilient, natural, and creative. Aspiring performers can find hope in her story, encouraging them to accept their pathways and speak up for others and themselves. Through sharing her life's lessons, obstacles, and victories, Christina has motivated many people to follow their passions, put their health first, and encourage those around them.

CONCLUSION

When one considers Christina Applegate's incredible path, it is clear that she had many notable successes and learned many priceless lessons over her life and work. Christina has continuously shown resilience in the face of personal and professional setbacks, from her early days in the entertainment business to her renowned actor and campaigner position. Her dedication to empowerment, authenticity, and creativity is evident in every stage of her life, leaving a lasting legacy for the coming generations.

Her capacity for constant self-reinvention emphasizes Christina's success in the business. Her ability to switch between somber roles in films like "Dead to Me" to humorous roles like Kelly Bundy in "Married... with Children" demonstrates her versatility and commitment to her work. She has broadened the opportunities for women in Hollywood in addition to entertaining audiences by embracing a variety of roles and genres.

Christina's story highlights the value of adaptability and flexibility in pursuing our passions. It serves as a reminder that success frequently necessitates a willingness to change and take on new challenges.

Furthermore, Christina teaches us a valuable lesson in vulnerability and strength through her candor about her personal problems, especially her fight with breast cancer. By sharing her story with the globe, she has encouraged many people to prioritize their health and brought attention to the value of early detection. Her advocacy work shows how individual struggles may serve as potent catalysts for positive change, inspiring others to embrace their journeys and look for support.

Through her successful profession and negotiating parenting challenges, Christina has shared essential knowledge regarding work-life balance. Her dedication to pursuing her career goals and being a present and involved mother shows how personal and professional goals may coexist. This dualism emphasizes the value of self-care, support networks, and setting priorities for the things that matter in life. Through her experience, Christina hopes to inspire future generations to pursue holistic success by highlighting the possibility of finding fulfillment in personal and professional relationships.

Christina Applegate's narrative is a tribute to the strength of fortitude, sincerity, and willpower. In addition to shaping her profession, her ability to overcome hardship with bravery and grace has inspired a group of admirers who see her as a ray of hope. The teachings from her experience serve as a reminder that success is not just determined by awards but also by the positive effects we have on other people's lives and our ability to persevere in the face of adversity.

Christina's life is an example of a journey full of successes and lessons discovered. Her devotion to her family and community, her support of health awareness, and her contributions to the entertainment business have a profound impact and will live on for many generations. Her tale serves as a reminder that every obstacle encountered presents a chance for personal development and that pursuing authenticity and passion can result in a genuinely fulfilling life. In addition to being a personal account, Christina Applegate's journey is an inspirational tale that inspires all of us to face our paths with grit, empathy, and steadfast resolve.

www.ingramcontent.com/pod-product-compliance
Lightning Source LLC
Chambersburg PA
CBHW050326230526
45471CB00005B/2375